MW00933858

Wisdom Speaks Vol. 1
John L. Solomon

<u>DEDICATION</u>

**This book is dedicated to the loving memory of
my late father John L. Solomon,
who gave me long lectures and
gave me a strong work ethic as well as
the knowledge to add value to myself...Miss you dad, Rest
in Love!**

ACKNOWLEDGMENTS

This project is created to enlighten, empower and motivate those in need of wisdom and inspiration. All praise and thanks to Jesus Christ the author of my faith and my life, His story is the best story.

Special thanks:

To all my friends and family that have reached out their hands, opened their hearts, and touched my life; thank you.

Contents

WISDOM SPEAKS Vol 1.

John L. Solomon

"Go after wisdom, not go after wise man because wise man shows only the path, he himself is not the path!"

Mehmet Murat Ildan

Introduction

One definition of wisdom is insight, knowledge, and good judgment. We are so quick to give up and throw in the towel when it seems like we can't handle the trial that offsets our environment. We make every excuse to let it stop us from moving forward, we let it intimidate us, and we allow it to take our power, to control us or take control away from us. We don't stop and look at it as something positive or as an opportunity to grow; we only seem to see the negativity. So, if with wisdom you have knowledge and insight into things that challenge you, then you can take authority over your situations. Even though you're going through, you must realize that we still have the power to stand and push through whatever the situation. God has given us the wisdom to endure the trials we face even as the Word says "endure hardness as a good soldier" and He will never give us more than we can bear without giving us tools, knowledge, and a way of escape or the power to overcome the challenge.

To go through a challenge means to endure a trial, weather a storm of life, suffer through tribulations, or simply to pay a price and going through seems to be something we all dread. Most of us want to obtain things in life but we struggle to endure the trials we must go through in order to obtain the goals that are set forth. We feel like it's too much for us to handle when we have to go through strenuous trials never realizing that the process of going through is what makes us stronger, makes us who we are and what we can and will become. It gives us the ability to get to the next level. The wisdom we receive from the lessons we learn when going thru, gives us the ability to handle the situation, prepares us for what we will need for our next level, and it makes us unstoppable. We have to start looking at our situations as positive things. It may not be easy to go through it but look at the rewards of wisdom after you come out. Furthermore, the Lord has never failed or failed me. Some things didn't go down the way I wanted them to or planned, but somehow it still worked in my favor and for my good. I was in a backslidden place several years ago from some bad experiences and I felt God was not fair, so I turned away with disappointment in my heart. A prophet came and spoke to me and said, "Consider your ways and neglect not your duty to God in any season. Nothing has prospered with you while you neglected your duty to God, and nothing will prosper you if you continue to neglect your duty to God."

He went on to say in so many words, nothing is as it seems! The man who seems to have everything has nothing and the man who seems to have nothing has everything. I thought to escape poverty by chasing after money and material things; and yet poverty still came upon me for not doing God 's will.

I began to surround and horde my life with things, but things instead place of God is trash and golden trash… is still trash. As my eyes began to open again and I came to myself, I assumed that I had been cheating God. However, the only one I was cheating and deluding was myself and those who loved me.

In God's beautiful restoration and renewal in the light of my redemption; my message to my fallen, struggling, wavering, and concerned brothers or sisters, in wisdom and love is, consider your ways. Examine yourself regularly, and neglect not your duty to God in any season, His mercy is infallible, His grace is matchless, and His ways are pass finding out. Yet with loving kindness, He knows how to beckon and draw us back to our first love!

He has empowered me greatly as His offspring and a son of God. Notwithstanding, He is God, I am inferior and He is superior, He is God, I am nothing in and of myself but I am not in myself, it's in Him I live, move, and have my being. Nothing is anything without Him. Good is not good without His presence, Love is not love without His presence, living is not life without His presence, this may be hard to digest but sinning is not even sin if He is not there. Everything is everything because He is the source of life and the light of life. The Lord lives and blessed be the rock of my salvation. All things are because of Him and come to fruition because He is the absolute and is worthy of all the praise and worship. Therefore, think on these things and let this mind be in you under the power that we are the offspring of the Father, heirs of God and joint heirs with Christ and no good thing will He withhold from His children. With men this is impossible, with flesh and blood this is impossible, but I'm not moved by flesh and blood because with God, my God, my Father, All things are possible!

Faith It Till You Make It

"Faith it till you make it" is the anti-phrase to what some would suggest in the form of *"fake it till you make it."* The concept *"fake it"* is used to give yourself a sense of being where you want to go and fooling yourself and others that you are already there, but the problem is that if you fake it, it sends a message of having something that you really don't and cannot sustain if challenged. So instead of faking it, faith it! Faith is more than just a word or concept that carries religious overtones as some may propose, allow me to explain. Napoleon Hill, the American Author of the acclaimed book, Think and grow rich, recommended in another of his great works, Law of Success; that imagination is a principal in personal success. The definition he used for imagination is; **"an act or process of forming a conscious idea or mental image of something never before wholly perceived in reality by the imaginer** (Laws of Success, pg381)**."** When we place

that definition next to the definition of faith, **"the substance of things hoped for, the evidence of things not seen,"** (Holy Bible, Heb11:1) you may see how the two seem similar:

Imagination: an act or process of forming a conscious idea or mental image of something

Faith: the substance of things hoped for

Imagination: never before wholly perceived in reality by the imaginer

Faith: the evidence of things not seen

From that success or business perspective, Faith it till you make it, can also be said in a business sense of; *imagine the idea until it feels real*. However, it must already be real to you on the inside! Dare to live your dreams!

I am taking you on a journey. The story was told of a balloon salesman on the street of New York City, who attracted new customers by releasing a balloon whenever his sales dropped. As the balloon takes off in the air, new customers are attracted and his business would pick up again. The balloons were of different colors, first a white one, then a red one and later a yellow one. After watching for some time, a little black boy asked the balloon salesman an insightful question. "Mister, if you released a black balloon, would it also go up?"

The balloon salesman looked at the little boy and said, "Son, it's what's on the inside of those balloons that make them go up, not their colors." Know this, it's what's inside you that will allow you to go up and make things happen! The things you want to experience and things you most desire must begin from within. If what you want most is not on the inside of you, no amount of hard labor can make it happen on the outside. To change your outer world, you must first change your inner world. Everything that happens in your physical reality comes from the inside. Your journey into the world of wealth and purpose, and love, and happiness begins with saturating your mind with thoughts of gratitude for what you already have. The thoughts of your mind will define or distort the perceived reality of what you want your life to look like.

Consequently, don't be discouraged along you journey of faith! You must let time run its course and bring the reaping season around. Manifestation does not happen overnight. The people, resources and circumstances you need must all revolve into their proper orbit and come into alignment. During this time of active waiting, continue in faith, knowing that your goals are already visible and that you are on your way to apprehending them.

"Consistency, thou art a jewel!" Shakespeare said. You must consistently work within your mind to create the desires of your heart and to do those quantifiable things that bring them to existence within the physical world. Manifestation requires persistent, insistent mental and emotional engagement. Therefore, visualizing your goals and thinking are incremental factors but you must also engage in affirmative action in the physical world to produce your dream, or idea, or nothing will happen because faith void of actions is dysfunctional.

~ **The ability to have the life we desire begins with an attitude empowered to push past our myths, doubts, and fears of who we once were and into the powerful present of our presence of who we now are and what we are able to accomplish.** ~

Be Valuable and Think

You are not an accident, an incident or a mistake regardless of how you were conceived or what situation you were born in. We are worth more than what the world values because you must not limit or quantify yourself by a monetary value that suggests you're worthless. Money should not make or define you, you should define and make money. You are the prize and of great value, YOU MUST BELIEVE THIS! Anything of material worth that you think is more valuable than you in essence, will never be affordable in your consciousness. Say this, "no material thing or substance is greater than I." Furthermore, you are not junk, you are not an afterthought, nor are you someone's frail opinion of what they think of you. I proclaim today that where others have looked down on you, overlooked you, or even tried to undermine your relevance, renounce that derision!

Now prepare for the greatness, the wealth, the wonder and the awakening of the incredible you to be chiseled out of the rock of disappointment; into a magnificent sculpture of promise. Why, because there is no individual on earth who is like You! Today is the day that you motivate yourself, inspire yourself, breakthrough your comfort zones and lift the lid on your capacity as you decide to become what you believe you have been destined and purposed to be! Again, it's time to become what we once only wished to be. In the word destiny, you see the word tiny because what you are destined to Be, starts out small or tiny. Accordingly, we despise not the day of small beginnings. Everything that is big was once small.

That tiny thing (YOU) has the potential to grow, mature and advance into the powerful being you realized you can be and make a difference, a contribution, or an impact on your environment, your community, your city, and even your world! Understand that the seeds of destruction are at the conception of a thing. Meaning, the events, environment, and vessels in which brought forth your conception; have the innate ability to destroy you. **Events**: what was happening around you as you were being formed in your mother's womb? **Environment**: what type of atmosphere surrounded you as you developed as a child? **Vessels**: who were the people of influence that had charge with your direct care and up bringing? These variables are important because they wrote a program or instructions within you that merged with what was already in your DNA. Take a close look at your programming and determine with the guiding of the Spirit (Romans 12:1,2) if you need to reprogram your thinking or instructions in order that you may BE what YOU were destined and designed to BE!

As an individual thinks, that is what he or she positions themselves to become. Your perception is not reality but rather a filter whereby you view reality, which you accept as your reality. Your perception presents a reality that is or is becoming an actuality as things in your physical environment line up with your personal and mental vision. Our thoughts then determine our life and state of being. What then forges my thoughts? Your Core values and grounded beliefs. Our core values and beliefs are the "juice" from which our thinking drinks. These values and beliefs fuel, influence, and or produce thoughts which then create, shape, and form the world around me.

I then interact with this environment I helped to form, through certain behaviors and produce circumstances and situations by my decisions and actions which are governed again by my core values and beliefs. Understand you may have been born into an environment of someone else's low-level thinking such as poverty, crime, sickness, slavery, abuse, or helplessness; but that does not determine you have to remain in those life stealing conditions. My state of mind and mental posture determines if I become, embody, and remain in those purgatoric or hellish conditions of living or do I encourage myself to do better and be better. I encourage myself to get up and do better, and moreover, do more than what I have done prior to get out of that situation and those circumstances. (Let me preach here)

Praise your way out, sing your way out,

power your way out, cry your way out,

fight your way out, love your way out,

laugh your way out, talk your way out

push your way out, pry your way out,

pray your way out, play your way out,

pay your way out, run your way out,

sweat your way out, jump your way out,

flip your way out, think your way out,

read your way out, educate your way out,

give your way out, scream your way out,

shout your way out,

stop-drop-and roll your way out...

Whatever works in retrospect to progressively get out of a bad situation which is destroying your higher sense of self and consciousness, you do it! You can choose not to conform to a low level of living in lack and self-destructive habits. You can transform your thinking with renewed beliefs, values, images and visions that will cause you to resonate and ascend to a higher plane of thinking, a higher calling, higher living and higher ways of being in the image of a God whose thoughts and ways are higher!

~ Your inward conversation creates your outward manifestation. The world is full of negative things and events that put you down and tell you what you cannot do or will not become, so become your own cheerleader. Tell yourself regularly, I think I can, I know I can!

Some Scars You Have to Show

We as a human race are obsessed with our appearance. So much money goes into hair and beauty care products, that the global beauty market reached $265 billion in 2017. This shows our demand for skin crème, foundation, anti-aging, blush, masks, moisturizers, serum, cleansers, oils, mascara, concealer, and sunscreens. Besides that, add on the 12 billion we paid in 2014 for plastic surgeries and the fact that a typical tanning salon will bring in between $150,000 and $300,000 per year. This further demonstrates that we put our money where our "appearance" is because we care about how we look. We prefer to hide or get rid of our rolls, our gray, our wrinkles, our cracks, our blemishes, our stretch marks, and our scars because we view them as ugly and reminders of our pain or our morbidity. But rather, in some cultures and contexts scars are signs of a warrior, a survivor, and or a miracle.

They may be ugly to some but let it be a badge of healing and an emblem of what was endured and overcome. One of Jesus disciples named Thomas didn't go for the cover-guy metro sexual make-over so he emphatically shared what he was thinking concerning Jesus being returned from the grave, "Except I see in his hands the print of the nails, and put my finger into the print of the nails, and push my hand into his side, I will not believe." Thomas as I call him, the apostle of Missouri-the show me state, and he was basically saying, "I want to see His scars with my own eyes or I won't believe it!" You may indeed walk by faith and not by sight which is a spiritual attribute and biblically sound, but there are many people who live by the mantra of "seeing is believing." That doesn't make them bad people, it's just that they require more concrete evidence and your word may not be enough.

It is for those types you pull out your paperwork, show them the receipts, let them view your pictures, take them to the building, let them meet people who were there, and show them your scars. Expose the scars for all to see and denounce the negating feelings or doubts by rerouting your mental energy to give God thanks for something presently good in your life. This redirects your attitude from a downward spiraling descent into an upward crescendo. Consequently, the negative feeling is absorbed by a new feeling of hope and revival as when a light is turned on in a dark room. There are still shadows of dark in a well-lit room, however, the overall gloom of darkness and helplessness is no longer magnified. Accordingly, don't focus on the shadows of darkness which are likened to the small lingering scars of the negative feeling; but focus on the creative power of your praise to create the positive powerful experience you want to manifest and impact your today. Be empowered and take responsibility for your circumstances. Too many people have a habit of blaming their circumstances or mistakes on other people, e.g. the devil, a curse, I'm being punished, or bad luck. The Lord speaks into your life and you have to execute God's will and not a religious ritual. It is only you that's left to foot the blame when you fail to execute the plan or claim the victory.

Understand that adverse issues may prompt you to hit the panic button and go out of character. Rather maintain your peace and prayerfully work through those trying times. Then get busy changing and rearranging your circumstances so that in your next season, you won't be in a place of pity, but will be in a position of power and the scars you show today will be badges or tattoos of what you have triumphed over!

~Where you are now, is not where you will always be if you choose to move to a better place beyond that place of doubt, confusion and chaos. Move into a place of, where I am is not who I am, I choose better for me. Now go there!

Never Underestimate Their Wiifm

There is a teaching tool that some professors in colleges use called a **WIIFM** (an acronym pronounced wiff-em). The letters stand for What's In It For Me and this tool is designed to show the pupil what they will receive and benefit from the lesson. What I have noticed is that some people in general live their lives in the WIIFM zone. If they do anything of value or less for you, they pull out their WIIFM card and suggest if not directly ask, what's in it for me?

There are still some good people who are good Samaritans and will help with no strings attached. These random acts of kindness and blessing of others are often lifelines that save us when we find ourselves in compromising, vulnerable, lonely, and hopeless situations.

The acts that you have done that you considered small, insignificant and forgot about, God did not forget.

As you have enriched the lives of others, out of the treasures of your own heart and wealth, you were really positioning yourself to be blessed by the good seeds and good acts that you have done. Your rewards, favor, and blessings are extensions of your own behavior. What you thought was insignificant, something great and larger than life was being stored up for you and you will be blessed more than you could ask because you didn't even consider the WIIFM. However, in the negotiations of business, contracts, and financial deals, you would be wise to question what is the WIIFM with the person or parties you are dealing with. They are not doing the deal simply for the love or out of the kindness of their heart. They have an expectation and an interest in dealing with you because there is something in it for them that they want. Therefore, don't be undersold, dummied down, or let your kind heart strings be tugged and you make an emotional deal for the sake of helping your buyers get a good deal that leaves you feeling like what a good saint you are. Remember business is business and people have a self-interest when they sit down at the negotiating table. This does not mean that you don't love donating to the kids, helping the poor, or feeding the less fortunate. It means that you are a shrewd business person who reads the fine print before you sign, who understands what holds value, and recognizes when people think your kindness means sucker. Not everyone is an opportunist out to dupe you or take advantage, but the reality remains, most have a WIIFM agenda card so never underestimate another person's tendency to seize their lion's share of your possessions My personal WIIFM is that I strive to move and operate in a higher realm of consciousness and understanding in the similitude of God when He declared my thoughts are more elevated than your thoughts and my ways are more established than your ways. Therefore, my mind turns upward to reflect the directives from heaven, this and each day without demonic interruption. From heaven I receive signals, unctions, images, and messages through the transparency of my spirit toward God and He reveals to my soul direction, regulation, understanding, solutions, and opportunities that are available for myself and God's elect people.

I am instructed and led by the Spirit of the Lord, He has given me the tongue of the learned and my lips speak wisdom treasures and fruitful paths of life. I transcend the physical obvious, I excel pass the popular mentality, I clear away disturbances, I increase the people of God in breakthroughs and I refuse the selfish status quo. I move around distractions to breakthrough into prophetic truths, to expose uncertainties and to foil evil operations, to decipher codes and coded language, to interpret dreams and visions, to extract wealth and to facilitate wealth transfers, and uncover apostolic revelation which is revealed to the student of Christ that studies to show themselves approved of the Lord. I AM the true priesthood and I am daily reminded of how my God supplies all my need according to His riches in glory, therefore the spirit of poverty is broken off of my life and all grace abounds toward me. I am linked and numbered among the children of God, intelligent people, who understand the signs of the times, well versed in life affairs, and know what is proper to be done in all the exigencies of human life.

Now, I am angelically and heavenly briefed of what is both the spiritual interest and civil duty of my family to advance the will and the Kingdom of God. I decree and declare that my name is placed on the mind of interceding watchmen who open doors for individuals to prosper, and my name is on the lips of worshipping key masters who escort and break individuals through to opportunities that were once locked in order that I may establish God's covenant for generations today and after me. My WIIFM is His will for my life being fulfilled and the people that love God! What is your WIIFM

in this life?

~ **If you don't go after what you want, you will
never have it. If you don't ask for it, the answer
is always no. If you don't will to step forward,
you will remain in the same place~**

Nora Roberts

Think and Proceed to Achieve

If you are thinking the worst, if you are thinking it's over, if you are thinking I am not able to do the things I need or want to do, then you are correct. The first obstacle you must deal with is your negative thinking. What you think about determines your attitude toward that thing thought about and your ability to accomplish or fail.

Prov 23:7 For as an individual thinks, corresponding to belief in their heart, so it is that this individual will have and or become.

Think about certain events in your life and try to remember what kind of thoughts you often had before a particular event happened. Try to establish a link between your thoughts and the events. How many times has something happened in your heart before it occurred and you perceived this was going to happen? Your dominant thoughts played a part in this because they influenced your behavior and therefore, attract people, things and events into your life. Not speaking that your thoughts were definitive causation of the event. However, there is a recognizable correlation. A determined and positive mind anticipates happiness and a successful outcome in every situation and action. Whatever the mind expects, it finds. Therefore, the next thing you must do is elevate your thinking to a higher level. What you choose to think about is up to you. You can't tell a bird not to land on your head, but you can stop it from building a nest there. In the same manner, all kinds of thoughts come to you but you don't have to process and ponder them unless you choose to do so. But understand that essentially thoughts have the creative ability to become things.

A social studies teacher of mine would say to my peers and I, "you can take a mule to water but you can't make him drink it; and in the same sense you can lead a fool to knowledge but you can't make him think it." Now had I

known any better, I should have been offended at the notion

that he called us both mules and fools in the same breath.

However, being the fools and mules, that we were, it did not

kick in till a few years later when I realized that what he was

saying to a group of immature 8th graders was that we were

too stubborn to drink or process the life knowledge we were

receiving which would lead to higher learning and under-

standing whereby we could accomplish our goals.

"Maybe it is time to consider living dangerously. Maybe it's
time to reject the commands of power, the dictates of society
and public norms that say you cannot. Stop worrying about
what is changing, what isn't working and what you don't like
about yourself. It's time to (think) and manifest what you
desire."— Dick Sutphen:

For some that statement is too liberating, it affords to

much freedom and may suggest anarchy. I am not suggesting

this statement to a people without knowledge, but I am pro-

posing this to a people who know their potential to take the shackles of monkey see monkey do, that go along to get along attitude off of their minds, and the limitations of past failures off of their lives.

Here's the formula (motive + ability = potential)

Motive is your reason or purpose to do or to go after a goal

Ability is your skill set and the capacity you have to operate optimally in that craft or talent

Potential is what is possible for you to achieve based on your motive and ability

That's why each component of the formula must be encouraged, empowered, and enhanced;

- **Encourage/motive**: promote and give assurance to an individual's purpose; some people just need a little push. **Encouraged motive produces boldness!**

- **Empower/ability**: authorize and sanction an individual to use their ability, some people are looking for and waiting on permission to operate. **Empowered ability amps up confidence!**

- **<u>Enhance/potential</u>**: help to develop and increase an individual's potential, some people need a little bit of mentoring and guiding to show them what they can achieve. **Enhanced potential creates belief to act with the efficacy to succeed!**

As you process this formula and employ it to level up your life, you will begin to operate with energy and an urgency that allows you to achieve your goals and produce the results that you want. My thoughts today are investments into what I will get on tomorrow, if I think that things will be chaotic today based on yesterday's pattern, even though every day is different, then it becomes a self-fulfilled prophesy.

Yes, observe patterns and prepare based on the possibility of what was learned from yesterday, but project success for today and forecast prosperity for tomorrow. Base it on God, base it on good, base it on the source of all things prosperous. Base it on putting God first according to His love and His law that all things will work together for my good. Don't let what happens to you in a negative sense get confirmed in your mind as a law or an order of normal operations for your life. This will produce and set up an internal and invisible roadblock that will impede your progress each time you set out to accomplish something purposeful. And this roadblock will project itself upon your physical environment making you think the obstacles are without when they are lying in wait hidden within.

~You must sow the seed of your desire and transform your mind to bring that which you desire into existence according to the parallel and equal laws of sowing and reaping upon your actions. You must then consistently meditate to cement the desires of your heart into your spirit and do those physical things that create a place to bring them into the material world. ~

If Your Feet Hurt, Take Off Your Shoes

Women will spend hours in a shoe store looking for the right pair of shoes to go with that outfit. She goes out that night on the set and dances and struts around the scene for hours. But somewhere in her bag or the car she has a pair of flat shoes waiting for the end of the night to slip out of those fine heels and into those flats because...her feet hurt!

More than often, we find ourselves in positions and places that are uncomfortable and cause us much stress. Why do we choose to stay in these painful, hurtful, and unfulfilling situations and or circumstances? Is it because we feel obligated or that we have no choice. My friend you always have a choice. It may not be easy to make a hard decision but if something is breaking you down, taking your under, vexing your soul, and causing much grief, don't stay there being miserable and should you choose to stay, STOP complaining and deal with it or plan your exit strategy.

There is always a familiar feeling for each of us associated with pain and discomfort. Some will embrace it while many seek to erase it. A feeling is produced by some thought or stimulant but don't avoid the feeling, rather feel it and discover the source that brought it. After discovery of the source of the thought or stimulant, find the goal of the source that produced the feeling and there you will find enlightenment on how to decrease or increase this feeling. We all experience feelings but some have been traumatized in their emotions by an incredible event and that event is a hollow place of pain that is fixated in the life of the person who has been wounded. There is healing for your hollow place today. That place where you have experienced great pain and suffering from some un-relivable event needs to be healed so that you may be whole in your life.

Some of us continue to live with the event and the pain of what happened reoccurring each time it is thought upon or triggered. We suppress this event, but anytime something happens in our life that resembles this event, an echo of pain is released from that hollow place in your soul. My mother said plainly to me one day as I brooded over a painful situation, "son, if your feet hurt, take your shoes off." Then you can see what's wrong, but as long as you are in those shoes, your feet will keep on hurting until you can no longer walk. Healing begins the moment we admit that we are or were hurt, wounded, injured, and in pain. Many walk around in denial that, "I am fine you are fine", but we are not fine. No, we don't confess negative, or complain uselessly but we must face a reality that we have been hurt and have to get over these wounds that cause us to hurt others and keep a perpetual cycle of hurt. A wounded animal becomes aggressive as you get close to their injury and we as humans become aggressive and lash out when someone gets close to our pain. We lash out because we fear they will hurt us more and bring greater pain so we fight and cover, so as to not appear weak and vulnerable to those that would inflict hurt. However, we are also pushing back those who could administer healing. A wound that stays covered in darkness does not heal properly. I have experienced and understand the difficulty in opening up and trusting someone when all you have known is judgment, ridicule, misunderstanding, and humiliation. Drugs, illegal or prescribed is not the panacea. Alcohol, another party, another sex partner, more money, and more fun and even religion may medicate or dull the pain. However, these things will not heal the deep wounds of rejection, abuse, molestation, loneliness, abandonment, and failure. Today is your Day, our day to get better! God is releasing healing at no charge and as we go to Him today, He is sending someone to us that will bring healing and answers to our issues and dis-ease.

Be mindful that your healing will not be or come how you will expect them or it to come but it is coming and already nearer than we know. Reject the notion that "I am fine you are fine", when healing and relief is in your proximity. At some point in our journey of life we must accept help to get over what has hindered and held us back or remain in the same drudgery and dysfunction. Lord heal me in my hollow place today and fill it so that the emptiness in that depressed area of my being may no longer be triggered by familiar circumstances and symbols. Let it be filled with your love that I may be restored and recover from the pain that once haunted me in my defeated hollow place.

~ If it hurts, then be in pain, if you get through
that hurt then strength you have gained! ~

Lead, Follow, Or Get Out of The Way

Leadership always declares itself and leadership never translates as anything less than leading. When it's time to lead no matter the occasion or situation, a true leader will do just that, emerge and lead, especially in tough times. If no one is following you, it is said that you are just taking a walk. It is good to reevaluate your leadership through some form of accountability and ask, am I being effective at doing my assignment? Many leaders are called to lead but do not want to answer to anyone and it is dangerous to be a leader of anything without checks and balances on earth. It is true that power corrupts and power unchecked will take those who have it down a dark path. Some of our leaders in business, government, education, and church do not want accountability. We have strayed away from wanting to have a check and balances deeming it unnecessary and outdated choosing popular opinion and education to support our independence from the process. Joshua had Moses, Elisha had Elijah, the 12 had Jesus, and Timothy had Paul, but yet our generation rejects its fathers and predecessors for a lame attempt to reinvent the wheel and come up with a new direction that has no roots. Yet under new the new school of leadership there are benefits today that we who are a bridge into the new generation need to understand.

Old Leadership Command	New Leadership Culture
Defensive minded	Offensive minded
Command and control	Influence and advise
Followers and servants	Partners and friends
Micro managing	Self-managing
Individual concept	Team concept
Pyramid leadership	360-degree leadership
Employees	Team members
Supervisors	Team leaders
Mechanical/Robotic	Innovators

A seasoned leader has submitted themselves to the process of many rites and instructions. He or she has borne ridicule, misunderstanding, rejection and criticism in the quest to apprehend their visionary destiny. He or she has been betrayed by a "Judas," and has agonized in their own personal Garden of "Gethsemane" where he or she had to decide between their own dreams and aspirations versus the greater good. He or she has endured the shame of "crucifixion," at some point, in the form of rendering an unexpected and undesirable sacrifice in order to complete and also compliment his or her walk of obedience to God and body of work they are chosen to lead. Indeed, a faithful experienced leader has paid a great price for the work and business of blessing others. However, your sacrifice will multiply into a great deal of extreme benefits that will be released from your account of integrity during a season in which you will reap reparations that will be overwhelming and demonstrate the goodness and faithfulness of God.

Leaders think differently than followers and their lives reflect it. The average person doesn't come to the end of a season and spend time reflecting on lessons learned and how to make the greatest impact in the following year. If you take the time to write out your thoughts, what you learned, the mistakes you made, and what you want to achieve in the season ahead, you have just separated yourself from the pack. What you think about matters. What makes you wonder? What captures your imagination? What do you dream about? What makes you angry? What do you want to change? These are the kinds of things leaders think about. Don't spend your time fussing about little things that don't matter. Things that make you a picky and petty person. People don't want to follow a picky and petty leader. People don't want to follow negative leaders. These types of leaders need to get out of the way as they are counterproductive and keep the members and the organization stuck in a cycle of counterproductivity. People desire and need to follow positive leaders with ideas of how to make life better and who have a heart for what the people need.

~ **If your acts arouse others to do more, live more, give more, be more, and you inspire others to speak up, come up, stand up, get up and never give up, you are a leader!** ~

Make It Happen

Whatever you want to be good at, you must exercise and practice and be diligent consistently. Practice does not make perfect, but your level of expertise in an area depends on the type of practice. Bad practice creates malpractice but perfect practice can make one perfect or a master in their field. Professionals and experts do habitually what amateurs and wannabes do casually. Become habitual in doing what you do best and you won't have to pretend to be ready when the light shines on you. Destiny is not maintained by one hit wonders but destiny is attained and sustained by those who continually attend to their craft or dream or desire. Your dream is that blessing, that benefit, that promotion, that goal, that high mark that you want to achieve! It is that vision that has not made it into your awakened life. It is that objective that keeps getting moved back. It is that promise you have yet to fulfill. It is that project that you have yet to complete. It is that wish of you wanting your fairy godmother to turn that pumpkin into a carriage so that you go to the ball Cinderella. I'm here to tell you Cinderella that the glass stiletto slipper you are waiting for is nothing more than the shoe on your feet. Get to stepping into your dream. Stop lying to yourself Pinocchio! Your dream is real and your faith in yourself to bring it to pass is what makes it more real. No more lies to yourself in the form of excuses as to why you can't make it happen. Stop your nose from growing, time to make your dream grow! Dumbo was in a predicament where he faced an awkward opportunity to fall and perish or flap his unusually oversized ears and fly. No, he didn't just fly, he soared! Understand the analogy here of Dumbo. The thing that you are sad about, mad about, ashamed of, misunderstood about, it is those big ears Dumbo that is going to cause you to fly and Go get IT! Now is the Time to forget about what you don't have and utilize that which you do have. No longer will you fret over what didn't work and direct your energy towards what you want and believe is going to work. Neither will you waste your power talking and thinking about what you don't want to happen because that is the very thing that will happen. The inverse of an idea is not stable enough to sustain your momentum to reach a goal in the long haul. Keep proclaiming and thinking over what you want to happen and the moves you are taking to Make it happen!

Your dream is not something you place on the shelf and wait for that elusive one day to happen. Your dream is that gigantic idea, that sleepless pursuit, or outstanding entity that you believe in and work at to make happen. Georgia Byrd in the movie "Last Holiday" proclaimed, "Next time... we will laugh more, we'll love more; we just won't be so afraid." Great advice but how about we get busy doing that NOW and not wait for next time, it may not be a next time! Go and set the pace to make it happen, now! Against all odds, upstart entreprenuers are making it happen. Against poor health reports, terminal illness patients are making it happen. Against domestic abuse and discrimination, women who were once beaten down are making it happen, senior citizens who were told it's too late for them, are making it happen! It's time to make it happen! Hard working single mothers are making happen, unsung devoted fathers are making it happen. Enthusiastic teachers are making it happen, 1st responders making it happen. Essential personnel making happen, everyday people making it happen! It is your dream and if you don't believe in it, no one can make It happen for you! But if you can believe today, if you can envision your dream, articulate your dream, not only will it happen, but it will happen and give birth to the dreams of others with a passion you never imagined possible!

Nevertheless, it will not come to pass by osmosis, you have to earn it! The power to make "IT" happen comes when your attitude elevates above your struggle. God provides a way of escape through hardships, but He told us he won't place more on us than we could bear. As a result, strength comes when you go through and endure the struggle. The easy way out of a struggle is a way of escape, if you need the escape, take it as it is there for you. However, the best way out of a struggle is to face it, learn from it, conquer it and conquer yourself in the process. Your dream is entrusted to you and it is not to be taken for granted or undervalued. Therefore, put your work in, get your 10,000 hours and become an expert in your field.

You must apply yourself and acquire the knowledge you need to make yourself formidable in the area of your dream. However, you don't have to go around asking everyone what to do or how do you do it when it comes to your dream. A lady had a reoccurring dream of being chased by a monster, one night in the dream the monster caught her and she screamed, "what are you going to do to me?" the monster replied, " Lady, I don't know it's your dream!" You get it? Don't wait for others to tell you what to do with it, IT'S YOUR DREAM! Go get it! Learn all that you can about what you need to be successful in your area and then once you have acquired the knowledge, strive to become the best. Then they will ask for you by name, because YOU have earned it!

~ Until you change on the inside you are obligated to live with what comes to you on the outside. Your inner magnet or thinking attracts to you the things you think of and speak about. ~

Find Your Power

A strong, hard punch to someone's jaw could knock them down or out, versus a small tap to someone's knee cap. However, if that small tap was delivered consistently to this person's knee cap in the same place over a long period of time, similar results would take place in the sense of knocking them down or stopping that person as would the strong hard punch; only not as epic and would take longer. This is how the enemy attacks us, he patiently taps the spot consistently over a long period time until it breaks down. We must not ignore the little frequent taps because they are not the haymaker knockout punch. If we underestimate the little taps, we will find ourselves knocked down and bewildered as to how it happened. In retrospect, as a forgone conclusion, if you allow your enemy to tap your vulnerability every day, he has subtly delivered the knockout blow. Because small gradual advances, without resistance will surely bring about the accomplishment of an intent. From another vantage point of the small tap, to the same place, consistently over a long period of time; it can produce wanted results when a monumental move is not possible in the present time. The small tap method requires disciple and patience as most are more willing to go for the illustrious colossal move over the small tap. Though the monumental or colossal move is less time consuming and produces instant results, the small tap method builds a greater resiliency and a more comprehensive understanding of the process. How did the slow and deliberate tortoise defeat the skilled and faster hare? Having neither quickness or agility within the arsenal of his grace. Consistent and steady was the virtue of his pace. Though his opponent's arrogance provided him opportunity and space, it was this his will and persistence that won him the race.

The way to win the race and become the champion is to find your power... *Carpe diem quam minimum credula postero* – "Seize the Day." Challenge Assumed Constraints *that have been placed upon you.* An <u>assumed constraint</u> is a belief, based on past experience that limits current and future experiences. An elephant tied to a pole as a baby with a heavy chain will not try to get free from something as small as a rope later in life as a 6-ton adult, this is an assumed constraint. Don't be hindered any longer by the chains of what THEY think is best for you. THEY are assumed constraints and restraints that keep us from moving forward because they believe and see something different for your life. It's your life to live and you are IN COMMAND of it! Don't be consumed by a wave of opinions from people who are doing nothing with their lives and squandering their opportunities. *Carpe diem*– "Seize the Day/ take hold of your today and find your place in the sun! You are a champion!

A champion is one who is the winner after a challenge or competition, one who comes through in a trying moment...considered a valiant warrior, a brave heart soldier, a mighty man or a powerful woman. Sometimes an ordinary person, doing an extraordinary thing! Head coach Rudy Tomjanovich gave us one of the most inspirational quotes after winning the 1995 NBA title when he Declared, "never underestimate the heart of a champion!"

A champion will fight and win against the odds, or even when outnumbered.
A champion knows he or she may have to stand alone with his or her back up against a wall.
A champion does not quit and give up in the face of fatigue but sticks to what works.
A champion will always defend his or her ground and protect those on his or her team.
A champion understands the assignment and delivers in spite of the opposition.

A champion believes in something greater than themselves.

A champion knows they are a champion before the battle begins.

Win or lose the champion knows he or she is still a champion.

 BE A CHAMPION …

~Winning is great, sure, but if you are really going to do something in life, the secret is learning how to lose. Nobody goes undefeated all the time. If you can pick up after a crushing defeat, and go on to win again, you are going to be a champion someday. ~Wilma Rudolph

Don't Wait Till It Is Raining To Fix

The Windshield Wipers

Do you find yourself putting on hold the things that you should be doing that will benefit your life and the Kingdom of God, but move more quickly on those things that will benefit others due to seemingly immediate circumstances and situations? Do you find yourself constantly starting projects but never finishing one before moving to the next? I asked God, "Why are so many of your people struggling financially, personally, physically, and spiritually?" The answer came, "My people are surrounded by situations and circumstances that weaken their faith, which cause them to hesitate in doing what they need to be doing or what I have asked them to do." God showed me that we are spending TOO MANY nights worrying, and wishing and hoping for financial miracles, things to work themselves out, and for

God to just intervene and do something! My people have areas in their lives that need adjustment from procrastination and stagnation. We are great starters, but terrible finishers. Paul said I stayed the course and I finished my assignment! Our enemy says, "we lack the discipline it takes to be a strong closer." I rebuke that statement and I rebuke distractions! WE have allowed the enemy to distract us from our NOW blessings in our NOW assignment! The spirit of fear, the spirit of doubt, the spirit of worry, and the spirit of frustration are the culprits who break our focus. These four destroyers tend to overwhelm us and cause us to get off track. Did you know that fear is NOT of God? Did you know that doubt is NOT of God? Did you know that worry is NOT of God? Did you know that frustration is NOT of God? Of course, you do. Yet the enemy is still trying to confuse us with thoughts that we do not have what it takes to make it. The adversary has one mission and one mission only - to kill, steal, and destroy. The enemy understands that you are God's workman here on earth; so, the only way to thwart the plan of God is by destroying YOU. If the enemy can keep you distracted and focused on what is NOT going right in your life and what is NOT happening in your life, you will never start USING WHAT YOU HAVE, TO GET DONE WHAT YOU NEED TO GET DONE FOR YOUR LIFE AND GOD'S PURPOSE!

We must not fall into the tapestry of reacting to situations only when they happen like fixing the wipers because it's raining. True we do have to manage emergencies and immediate crisis but we also have to be proactive because we know that it will rain again, so we have to think ahead and repair any problems before the rain comes.

I decree and declare," no more wasting of our time! No more wasting of our resources! No more dead-end jobs!

No more dead-end relationships! I refuse to travel down another dead-end road!" No more searching on the outside of myself to find that which God has already placed within Me. We have to start "using what we got, to get what GOD wants!" Today we fight against distractions, doubt, worry, fear and frustration and we become determined to get done what god wants, not by might, nor by power, but by the spirit of the lord who dwells within us!"

~You ask for rain, you gotta deal with the mud too. That's a part of it. ~Denzel Washington

Every breaking point has a breaking point

I know what the songwriter said "…oh what peace we often forfeit oh what needless pain we bear, we should never be discouraged take it to the lord in prayer." Unfortunately, you are going to have discouragement but here's the danger in the wrong attitude and staying in the wrong attitude.

1. when we don't have the right attitude, we view the world and our past and present experiences negatively.

2. When this happens, our bad attitude attacks our self-image and we began to bask in self-pity, self-blame and we demoralize our self-worth.

3. Next our negative attitude if unchecked becomes the glasses through which we see everyone else, so now we are

hating, criticizing, fussing and biting, and mad with every-one who is not paying us any attention, living their life and not being miserable like some of us.

4. Our bad attitude now begins time travel to prophecy how bad and worse things are going to get for our future and send us into a place of hopelessness and unconscious demonic control. If you are saying and agreeing with everything the devil says you are under demonic influence. You have to de-mand, come out my situation and get behind me Satan, you have no authority here!

It's time to stop making a bad day and a dark day, a dark life that blames everybody for your pain, your dilemma, and fight in life. Some say I blame me; it's now a suicide mission to turn the blame on yourself and shoot your self-worth that breaks down your spirit. You have to be made aware that **WEEPING MAY ENDURE FOR A NIGHT,** and you are going to encounter things in this life where you feel weak, defenseless, and have no control… build a bridge! You will get depressed when you are pressed by the pressure…build a bridge. Momma and everybody in your family from Kunta to Auntie Em struggled with something you are fighting to break the cycle from…build a bridge. You may go through worried about your appearance, your weight, your hair, your age, your status …build a bridge, and get over it, somebody likes it! Some days you as well as others are not going to have things go your way...build a bridge and at some point, get over it! Because life will move on with or without you, not being insensitive to grief or pain but others around you at some point move on and you must as well.

When you have to ENDURE for the night, you have a correct self-definition of who you are. Your ability to deal with disappointment, rejection, obstacles, and even temporary failure and setbacks determine the level of success you can achieve. If you can properly deal with these things: self-sabotaging characteristics, petty misunderstandings, back-stabbing friends, and people who resist your efforts to pro-gress, you can find your success formula and achieve any-thing. Because when you have reached your breaking point, the thing which is about to break you also has a statute of limitation meaning it has a point in which it will break also. The late great Gospel artist, Rev. Clay Evans told us to reach beyond the break and hold on!

~Every object has a shatter point, a limitation to its tensile strength; apply enough force, and it will break. ~ V.E. Schwab

See the Change Be the Change

"You must be the change you want to see in the world."

"As human beings, our greatness lies not so much in being able to remake the world – that is the myth of the atomic age – as in being able to remake ourselves."

Mahatma Gandhi

If you sense change on the rise, then most likely the winds of change are blowing in your direction. It is often quoted, "change yourself and you will change your world", but what if your world around you is rapidly changing? Before we answer that question consider this; if scientist and archeologist are correct, then the colossal behemoths known as dinosaurs once ruled and reigned supreme on earth. Now if that is true, where are these animal kings of the earth today? We don't see them so we believe them to be extinct. Now the golden question, why are they extinct? There are theories of meteors falling to earth and natural selection but on a social level we could interject on the surface, this not having to do with specific theory of direct cause but rather a basic component that life demonstrates through these is that, dinosaurs did not change or adapt to the new conditions in their environment so they died out or became extinct. We as people being creatures of habit, routine, and traditions; do not like to shift or tip over our sacred cows. Therefore, things pretty much stay the same until a revolution within a new generation breaks out to overthrow or fades out the old guard. Being so heavily set in our ways is a curse when change begins to happen all around us. We find ourselves trying to function in a world just like we always have, but the rules of procedure and operations have changed.

If we refuse to change, then just like the dinosaurs, we too will become extinct because our ways, language, knowledge, and understanding having become outdated; leaving us on the outside looking in.

Therefore, if you change how you think when you see a new wave coming, then you will change how you feel and what actions you take. And as the world around you changes, you won't be left behind. "Not only because you are now viewing your environment through new lenses of thoughts and emotions but also because the change within can allow you to take action in ways you normally wouldn't have or maybe even have thought about while stuck in your old thought patterns."

~You have to change with the change, it's not wise to remain the same when life insists that you make a change. ~

ABOUT THE AUTHOR

John L. Solomon Jr. was born in Macon, Ga to John and Jessie Solomon on Feb 2, 1970, the oldest son of four children. He is a decorated veteran of the United States Navy. He received an Associate's degree in Religious Studies from Logos Christian College, a bachelor's degree in Education from Regency College and a Psychology degree from Capella University. John has been an educator for three public school systems with behaviorally challenged and special needs students.

Solomon founded and established Life Altering Ministries, a ministry that empowers people to improve their thinking, increase the quality of their lives, and transcend their limitations. Today, John is currently living in Atlanta, GA.

In 2011, he a published The Eagle Who thought He was a Chicken. John's book gained much regional success and he was a national speaker for PA east coast author's conventions. His book speaks to youth to understand the uniqueness of their identity and calls to the potential in all of us to reach its peak. He followed this with, The Power Keys: Life of Wisdom, Job Interviews of a Different Kind, and Rooks the Fox who had no Tail. All on Amazon.com

He is the father to Zoe E'naiyah and husband to Antoinette Pizzaro Solomon.